NOTE T

Learning to read is an important skil
you can help your child reach. The A.
Reader program is designed to support you and your child through this process.
Developed by reading specialists, each book in the series includes carefully
selected words and sentence structures to help children advance from beginner
to intermediate to proficient readers.

Here are some tips to keep in mind as you read these books with your child:

First, preview the book together. Read the title. Then look at the cover. Ask your
child, "What is happening on the cover? What do you think this book is about?"

Next, skim through the pages of the book and look at the illustrations. This will
help your child use the illustrations to understand the story.

Then encourage your child to read. If he or she stumbles over words, try some
of these strategies:

- **use the pictures as clues**
- **point out words that are repeated**
- **sound out difficult words**
- **break up bigger words into smaller chunks**
- **use the context to lend meaning**

Finally, find out if your child understands what he or she is reading. After you
have finished reading, ask, "What happened in this book?"

Above all, understand that each child learns to read at a different rate. Make
sure to praise your young reader and provide encouragement along the way!

Introduce Your Child to Reading
**Simple words and simple sentences encourage beginning readers
to sound out words.**

Your Child Starts to Read
**Slightly more difficult words in simple sentences help new readers
build confidence.**

Your Child Reads with Help
**More complex words and sentences and longer text lengths help
young readers reach reading proficiency.**

Your Child Reads Alone
**Practicing difficult words and sentences brings independent readers
to the next level: reading chapter books**

9709 60 th Ave. South
Seattle, Wash. 98118

For Pam and her grandchildren, Amelia, Dashel, and Leo.
May your growing pod leap, swim, and play together like dolphins.

—C.R. and P.R.

Photo credits
Cover/title page: © Debra McGuire/iStockphoto.com
Pages 4–11: © Augusto Stanzani/Ardea; 12–13: © Charlie Phillips/age fotostock;
14–15: © Kevin Schafer/Alamy; 16–17: © František Czanner/iStockphoto.com;
18–19: © Auscape/Ardea; 20: © George Clerk/iStockphoto.com; 21: © Steve Bloom Images/Alamy;
22: © Valerie Taylor/Ardea; 23–25: © François Gohier/Ardea; 26–27: © Augusto Stanzani/Ardea;
28–29: © Blair Howard/iStockphoto.com; 30–31 © Tom and Pat Leeson/Ardea;
32: Photo by Molly Leff © American Museum of Natural History.

STERLING CHILDREN'S BOOKS
New York

An Imprint of Sterling Publishing
387 Park Avenue South
New York, NY 10016

STERLING and the distinctive Sterling logo are registered trademarks of
Sterling Publishing Co., Inc.

Library of Congress Cataloging-in-Publication Data Available

Lot #:
2 4 6 8 10 9 7 5 3 1
04/11
Published by Sterling Publishing Co., Inc.
387 Park Avenue South, New York, NY 10016

www.sterlingpublishing.com/kids

Distributed in Canada by Sterling Publishing
C/o Canadian Manda Group, 165 Dufferin Street
Toronto, Ontario, Canada M6K 3H6
Distributed in the United Kingdom by GMC Distribution Services
Castle Place, 166 High Street, Lewes, East Sussex, England BN7 1XU
Distributed in Australia by Capricorn Link (Australia) Pty. Ltd.
P.O. Box 704, Windsor, NSW 2756, Australia

Sterling ISBN 978-1-4027-8563-4 (hardcover)
978-1-4027-7784-4 (paperback)

For information about custom editions, special sales, premium and
corporate purchases, please contact Sterling Special Sales
Department at 800-805-5489 or specialsales@sterlingpublishing.com.

Designed by Amy Wahlfield

FREE ACTIVITIES & PUZZLES ONLINE AT
http://www.sterlingpublishing.com/kids/sterlingeventkits

AMERICAN MUSEUM
OF NATURAL HISTORY
EASY READERS

Baby Dolphin's
FIRST DAY

Peter and Connie Roop

STERLING CHILDREN'S BOOKS
New York

A baby dolphin is born in the ocean.

His mother takes care of him.

They swim together.

Dolphins must breathe air.

The baby dolphin takes his first breath.

He breathes through a blowhole.

It is on top of his head.

The mother dolphin whistles

to her baby.

The baby learns his mother's call.

He swims close to her.

The baby dolphin will soon learn

to whistle back.

The baby dolphin is hungry.

He drinks milk from his mother.

The mother is hungry, too.

She has found a fish to eat.

Dolphins live in every ocean.

Some dolphins live in rivers, too.

These are Amazon river dolphins.

Dolphins are some of the smartest animals in the water.

Dolphins swim together.

Their group is called a pod.

The pod swims fast.

The dolphins jump into the air.

They land in the water.

SPLASH!

Danger! There is a shark!

The baby swims closer to his mother.

The dolphins swim away.

The baby is safe.

A dolphin swims next to the baby
and his mother.

She helps care for the baby.

She is the baby's "aunt."

The dolphins swim almost all day long.

They leap. They dive. They move.

The baby needs to rest.

Dolphins take many short naps.

Dolphins must be awake to breathe.
They must swim to the top of the ocean
to breathe air.

The sun sets.

Baby dolphin's first day ends.

Tomorrow will be another busy day.

MEET THE EXPERT!

My name is **Neil Duncan**, and I am a biologist. I work for the Division of Vertebrate Zoology at the American Museum of Natural History in New York City. As a collections manager, I get to work with all kinds of animal specimens that have been gathered from around the world.

The natural world has always been a passion of mine, and I have traveled all over the United States to study animals. In California, I researched small forest mammals called fishers and martens; I helped protect endangered shorebirds from human disturbance and from predators in New York; and I have studied many other wildlife species, including fish and whitetail deer.

I received my Bachelor of Science degree in Wildlife and Fisheries Biology from the University of Vermont, and now I am earning my Master's degree from Hofstra University in New York. I am currently studying a species of turtle called the diamondback terrapin. I enjoy learning about diamondback terrapins because they are strong and hardy creatures, and they have managed to survive right near New York City.

If you are interested in biology, one thing you could do is volunteer for a local wildlife organization to learn what kind of animals live in your area. The world of animals is fascinating!